Genre Expositor

Essential Questio
What benefits come from people working as a group?

The Power of a Team

BY MARIA GILL

Introduction

Have you ever noticed how much easier it is to figure out problems when you work with other people? Sometimes you get so close to a puzzle that you miss a piece. It may be obvious to someone who's looking at it with fresh eyes. Other times, you have done all you can on your own. You need people with new skills to finish things off. Science is just the same.

There are thousands of scientists around the world who work together in teams to answer difficult questions. Some teams might be looking for a cure for a disease. Others could be finding ways to discover more about space.

Scientists often work together to solve problems.

People from different fields, or areas of knowledge, can produce powerful results when they collaborate. Physicists, biologists, and geologists may be researching different aspects of the same problem. By sharing their research findings and ideas, they can reach solutions a lot faster.

A TEAM EFFORT

Australian scientist Howard Florey was one of the first to gather a team of scientists. He wanted to find better ways of treating infections, and he saw that this problem was too big to solve on his own.

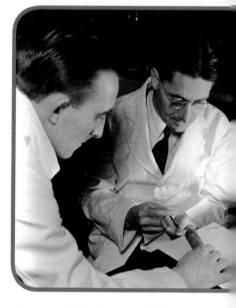

The team thought that penicillin could be the answer. Each scientist researched the uses of penicillin in his area of expertise, and the team shared their discoveries. Their results were so positive that penicillin was soon used to help sick children and injured soldiers. The team had found a cure for many common illnesses.

Howard Florey and his team saved thousands of lives.

Chapter 1
New Frontiers

When you're working on something as large as space, it pays to have plenty of brainpower on board. That's why scientists at **NASA** work in teams.

One team spent three years planning, building, and launching two robots to explore Mars. The robots would rove, or travel, across the planet. They would scan rocks and soil and send data back to Earth. However, before liftoff, the team had to find a place to land the robots safely.

One hundred Mars experts studied images of the planet and discussed their findings. Finally they picked two sites where there might once have been water. The first robot lifted off in June 2003 and the second in July 2003.

The two robots were named *Spirit* and *Opportunity*. The names were chosen from 10,000 entries in a student essay contest. This is *Opportunity*.

About seven months later, the robots reached Mars. The excited team watched the rover called *Spirit* touch down. Everything seemed to go smoothly, but then the engineers detected a problem. One of the **air bags** from *Spirit*'s **lander** was blocking the rover. Luckily, they had already figured out what to do if this happened. The driver in the control room turned *Spirit* sideways and drove it down a side ramp instead.

Three weeks later, the second rover, *Opportunity*, landed safely. Then the team could relax. More than three years of hard work had paid off.

The Mars Exploration Rover team gets the news that *Spirit* has arrived safely.

During the next few months, the scientists watched *Spirit* travel over rugged terrain. Its back wheel burst, but the team found a way for the rover to keep going. Sometimes they had to drive it in reverse with its damaged wheel dragging.

Then *Spirit* got stuck in the dirt. The team set up a sand trap back on Earth to mimic *Spirit*'s problem. Experts studied a model of the stuck robot and offered solutions. The team then tried out these possible solutions with the model.

Freeing *Spirit* actually led to one of the mission's most exciting discoveries. As its back wheel dug deeper into the dry soil, *Spirit* churned up a substance called silica. The presence of this substance told the scientists that there had once been water on Mars.

Team members use a model rover to figure out how to get *Spirit* unstuck on Mars.

After nearly two years of roving around Mars, *Opportunity* reached the edge of a large **crater**. The rover spent nearly a year exploring Victoria Crater's ancient, exposed rock. The data it sent back will teach geologists more about the history of Mars.

Opportunity roved from crater to crater, and in August 2011, it reached the rim of the giant Endeavour Crater.

Spirit stopped sending signals back to Earth in 2010. *Opportunity* is still roving across Mars.

A NASA EXPERIENCE

Thirteen teams of lucky high school students and teachers worked with the Mars Exploration Rover scientists during the rovers' launches and landings. The students were taking part in the Athena Student Interns Program. They woke up at 4:00 A.M. for team meetings, were given jobs to do, and attended press conferences.

Imagine what scientists might learn if other rover robots could analyze the rocks on Mars in more depth. The next rover mission sent a new type of robot called the Mars Science Laboratory to the planet. This robot is the size of a car. It's twice as long and three times as heavy as the first two robots.

This robot, named *Curiosity*, left Earth in November 2011. It landed on Mars on August 6, 2012. It discovered an ancient streambed, which prove that water flowed on the surface of Mars. It is truly a mobile laboratory, with tools for collecting and analyzing rock and soil samples. And NASA is working with the **European Space Agency** on an even bigger mission. They hope to one day bring samples from Mars back to Earth.

This is an artist's rendition of *Curiosity*. It has a laser to vaporize rocks so their dust can then be analyzed by special instruments.

Scientists at Bell Labs are also intrigued by the mysteries of space. One of the most important breakthroughs in the study of the universe came from two scientists there. The surprising thing is that what they found wasn't what they were looking for.

In 1964, Arno Penzias and Robert Wilson were using a huge microwave antenna to study radio waves in space. They kept hearing an annoying sound, like static. No matter where they pointed the antenna, it still picked up the noise. Finally they noticed bird droppings. Aha, they thought! They cleaned out the antenna and shooed away the birds. But the annoying sound remained.

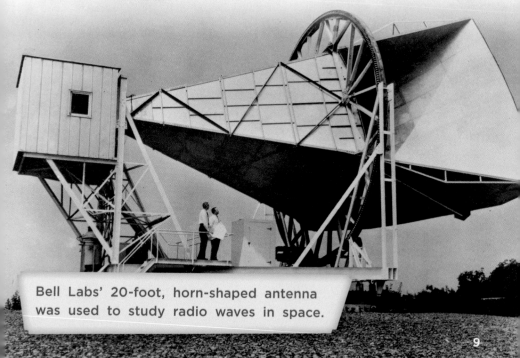

Bell Labs' 20-foot, horn-shaped antenna was used to study radio waves in space.

At the same time, Princeton University scientists were studying the **big bang theory**. This is the theory that the universe was formed by a huge explosion. Scientists believed the explosion would have left low-level **radiation** throughout the universe. When the two groups talked, they realized that this was what the antenna was picking up. It proved to the Princeton scientists that their theory was correct.

That "annoying sound" is now called cosmic microwave background radiation. In 1978, Arno Penzias and Robert Wilson won the **Nobel Prize** for their accidental discovery.

A SMALL INVENTION WITH A BIG IMPACT

In the 1940s, the technology behind long-distance phone calls was unreliable. Bell Labs scientist William Shockley wanted to make telephone signals stronger, so he assembled a team of physicists, chemists, and engineers. After two years of frustrating failure, they wrapped gold foil around a small plastic triangle that was touching a mineral called germanium. When they sent an electric signal through the device, the signal came out much stronger on the other side. Success at last!

Some more work led to the device the team called a transistor. They shared a Nobel Prize for their efforts, and transistors are now used in almost all electronic equipment.

The scientists at Bell Labs are still looking for ways to improve everyday life. They would like people to be able to communicate faster and more easily.

One team thinks the human body's central nervous system may hold the key. This system controls the heart, breathing, and body temperature. It helps our bodies to adapt to changes around us without our having to think about it.

When you surf the Internet or make a phone call, you use what's called a communication network. A network is equipment that is linked together. When you punch in a friend's phone number, the network picks up this signal and carries it to his or her phone. That's like the nerves in your skin sending a message through your nervous system to tell your brain that you are cold.

Humans love to communicate.

Our bodies send signals to our brains without our having to tell them to. But communication networks need human help, especially when they get lots of signals at once. Sometimes they can jam, such as when many people at an event are trying to use their cell phones at the same time.

Bell Labs wants to invent flexible networks to handle this sort of pressure automatically. The team working on this project has experts in math, computing, and engineering. Some are in the United States, and others are in France, Germany, and Ireland.

People want to connect anytime, anywhere as fast as possible.

Sometimes people work together because they are curious about the same thing. Other times, they are part of a business that wants to build a new product. And sometimes their reasons are personal. That's the case with The Miami Project.

Marc Buoniconti was just 19 when his spine was crushed during a football game. The injury was so bad that he was paralyzed from the neck down. Marc's father, Nick, wanted his son to walk again. Nick helped to set up The Miami Project. Marc is now president of The Miami Project and The Buoniconti Fund, which raises money for the project.

Marc and Nick Buoniconti have raised millions of dollars for spinal research.

SPINAL CORD INJURIES

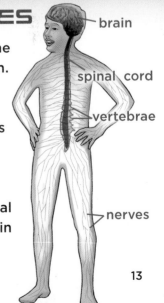

brain

spinal cord

vertebrae

nerves

Signals from our nerves travel through the body and up the spinal cord to the brain. The brain also sends signals down the spinal cord to the body. The spinal cord is a bundle of nerves protected by bones called vertebrae. When we see a great baseball catch, our brain sends a signal down the spinal cord to nerves in our hands, telling us to clap. But Marc's spinal cord was so badly damaged that his brain could not communicate with his body.

13

More than 200 researchers around the world work on The Miami Project. Some are figuring out how to prevent spinal cord damage. Others are looking at how to repair the spinal cord. One team is working on how to help patients recover.

The team has a theory about cooling the body down right after a spinal cord injury. They think it helps prevent more damage. They tested their theory by having doctors lower their patients' body temperatures for 48 hours. Then patients were slowly re-warmed by just one degree every eight hours.

The team found that these people had more movement after one year than is usual for people with these kinds of injuries. They are now planning to do a much bigger **trial** with hundreds of patients.

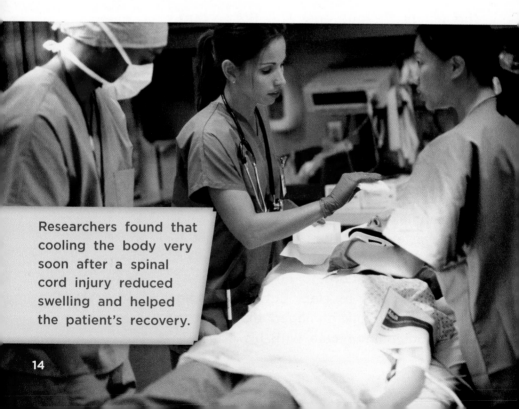

Researchers found that cooling the body very soon after a spinal cord injury reduced swelling and helped the patient's recovery.

The Miami Project's scientists also have theories on how to repair spinal tissue. One theory is that injecting special cells into a damaged area will help to fix it. These cells, called Schwann cells, have an important function. They make a substance called myelin. This wraps around our nerves like **insulation** around wires. The myelin helps the nervous system to communicate.

Researchers tested their theory on paralyzed rats. The rats regained 70 percent of their ability to walk. The results were so successful that scientists are planning a small trial with human patients.

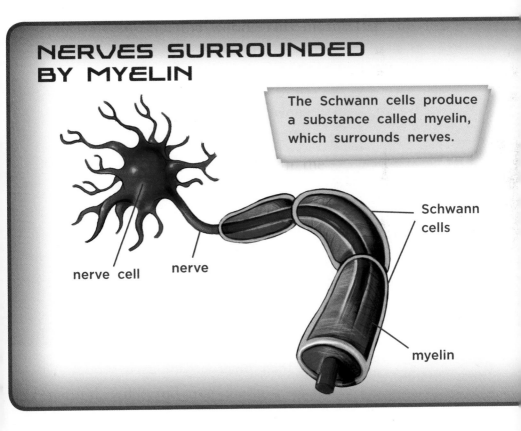

NERVES SURROUNDED BY MYELIN

The Schwann cells produce a substance called myelin, which surrounds nerves.

Schwann cells

nerve cell

nerve

myelin

Other researchers with The Miami Project are looking at how exercise using walking machines can help recovery. Still others are working on techniques to reduce patients' pain.

The Miami Project's scientists found that combining different treatments can also improve recovery. Teams in separate research areas are working toward one goal. They are dedicated to helping people with spinal injuries walk again.

Dr. James McClurkin wants to get robots to cooperate and take cues from their environment.

ROBOT TEAMS

What if we sent a team of 200 robots to Mars, instead of just two? How much more could we learn? Dr. James McClurkin would like to know the answer. He spends his time working on multi-robot swarms: groups of robots working together as a team.

The robots use infrared transmitters to share information. This helps the group stick together and react to changes in their environment. Dr. McClurkin says that his work was inspired by the teamwork of honeybees, which share information and respond to events in their environment as a group.

Conclusion

When scientists and experts work together, they can make faster progress and get better results.

What was a pesky noise to the scientists at Bell Labs turned out to be a missing piece in the big bang puzzle. William Shockley perfected the first transistor by building on the work of colleagues. Hundreds of people worked together to put the rovers on Mars.

By sharing ideas and results, scientists can make huge advances. One day, they may be able to bring rocks back from Mars. Or they may help people thought to be paralyzed for life to walk again.

Kids can experience the power of a team, too!

Summarize

Use important details from *The Power of a Team* to summarize the selection. Information from your graphic organizer may help.

Main Idea
Detail
Detail
Detail

Text Evidence

1. How can you tell that *The Power of a Team* is expository text? **GENRE**

2. What is the main idea of the second paragraph on page 4? Give key details to support your answer. **MAIN IDEA AND KEY DETAILS**

3. Look at the word *terrain* on page 6. It includes the Latin root *terr*, which means "earth." Use the meaning of this word part and context clues to figure out what *terrain* means. **LATIN ROOTS**

4. Write the main idea of each paragraph on page 14. Give examples of the key details that helped you determine each main idea. **WRITE ABOUT READING**

Compare Texts

Read how a team developed a special steering wheel.

HANDS ON THE WHEEL

Six student scientists, the Inventioneers from New Hampshire, have teamed up to produce great results. The students were challenged to prevent drivers from becoming distracted. Their work was part of a program in which students solve problems using research robots.

The students' work had many stages. First, they researched transportation safety problems. They found that New Hampshire had just banned texting while driving. They soon found that there was no device to correct distracted drivers.

Texting while driving is dangerous. The students aimed to prevent this type of unsafe driving.

19

Next, they observed the actions involved in texting while driving. They noticed that drivers held the wheel in a certain way when they were texting. After that, the team discussed how to solve the problem.

Their solution was a device that beeps when drivers hold the steering wheel in an unsafe way.

They built several models. Later they worked with the Massachusetts Institute of Technology (MIT) on a pilot study using an artificial driving machine. After they improved the model, they were able to promote their product to the car industry.

The team spent thousands of hours working on the project and built eight models. They were told that the beep in an early model was too quick and loud. It actually distracted drivers! They fixed that problem. They also made their product wireless so there were no wires to catch drivers' fingers.

HOW IT WORKS

The invention is a steering-wheel cover that can be fitted into any vehicle. The cover has sensors around its edges that can tell where a driver's hands are positioned on the wheel. The data is sent to a microcontroller, a very small computer. If the position is unsafe or if a driver's hands are off the wheel for too long, the device beeps and flashes lights to refocus the driver.

The super-smart six won the challenge. Now they have applied for a **patent** to protect their invention, the SMARTwheel™.

The team doesn't want any obstacles to get in the way of their invention being manufactured and sold. They believe their invention will help to reduce the number of car crashes.

An Inventioneer examines a SMARTwheel™ prototype.

Make Connections

Who did the Inventioneers work with to design their steering wheel? ESSENTIAL QUESTION

The scientists in *The Power of a Team* and the Inventioneers worked in groups on their projects. What did the teams have in common that helped to make their projects successful? TEXT TO TEXT

Glossary

air bags *(ayr bagz)* giant bags that inflate to cushion a lander's landing on Mars *(page 5)*

big bang theory *(big bayng THEER-ee)* the theory that the universe was formed from a huge explosion *(page 10)*

crater *(KRAY-tuhr)* a bowl-shaped depression caused by a volcanic eruption or by an object such as a meteorite slamming into the ground *(page 7)*

European Space Agency *(yoor-uh-PEE-uhn spays AY-juhn-see)* an organization set up by a group of countries in Europe to explore space *(page 8)*

insulation *(in-suh-LAY-shuhn)* a coating that prevents heat, movement, or sound from escaping *(page 15)*

lander *(LAN-duhr)* a protective spacecraft carrying the rover robot *(page 5)*

NASA *(NA-suh)* National Aeronautics and Space Administration, the United States' space exploration agency *(page 4)*

Nobel Prize *(noh-BEL prighz)* an international award given for major advances in knowledge *(page 10)*

patent *(PAT-uhnt)* a way of legally protecting an invention so nobody can copy it *(page 21)*

radiation *(ray-dee-AY-shuhn)* waves of energy sent out by sources of heat or light, including the sun *(page 10)*

trial *(trighl)* an experiment to test whether a theory is correct *(page 14)*

Index

Focus on Science

Purpose To show how a team can come up with a plan for a product using inquiry and technology

Procedure

Step 1 ▶ With a partner or a small group, brainstorm a problem you would like to solve using technology.

Step 2 ▶ What kind of product could you produce to solve this problem?

Step 3 ▶ Think about the kinds of people or knowledge you will need on your team to be successful.

Step 4 ▶ Make a product proposal. Draw your product. Include a description about what the product will do, why it's needed, and who you need on your team.

Conclusion To do something well, it is almost always better to work as a group because you get the knowledge and skills of each member of the team. What are some of the other benefits of teamwork?